D1808044

WATFORD GRAMMAR SCHOOL

Fuller Memorial Library

Acc'n No. 39353	Class'n OS 629.133

To be returned by:-

4 Jan 2018.

2 6 JUN 2018

22 OCT 1992

~5 NOV 1993

10 FEB 1995

2 0 OCT 1998

1 NOV 2006

1 1 NOV 2009

~ 6 SEP 2012

4 SEP 2013

WITHDRAWN

WATFORD BOYS' GRAMMAR

R03546W0622

Editorial: Steve Parker
Design: David West
Children's Book Design
Picture research: Cecilia Weston-Baker
Consultant: S J M Greene, British Aerospace

© Aladdin Books Ltd 1987

Created and designed by
N.W. Books

First published in
Great Britain by
Franklin Watts
12a Golden Square
London W1

ISBN 0 86313 627 3

Printed in Belgium

Contents

ENGINEERS AT WORK

AIRLINER

NIGEL CAWTHORNE

WATFORD GRAMMAR SCHOOL
FULLER MEMORIAL
39353   LIBRARY   OS 629.133

GLOUCESTER PRESS
London · New York · Toronto · Sydney

AIRLINER

In our modern world, engineering and technology are becoming more and more complex. Researchers develop new metals, plastics and other materials. Electronic specialists use computers in design, and to operate the finished product. Customers buying the product demand lower running costs, better reliability, and increased safety. Manufacturers must keep up with changing fashions, fulfil their customer's needs, and stay ahead of their competitors.

At the centre of design and construction are the engineers. Their work today will solve the problems posed by tomorrow's great buildings and giant machines, from skyscrapers to bridges, tunnels, motorways, power stations, cars – and airliners. The airline business is one of the most hi-tech and competitive of all. When a manufacturer plans a new airliner he must decide what his customers, the airline companies, need. A large plane, or a small one? Fast and expensive, or slow and cheap? Long-range or short-haul? Thousands of jobs, and millions of dollars, hang in the balance.

Today's airliner

The basic shape of a medium-sized airliner, like the Airbus A320 shown here, has changed little in the past 30 years. Passengers sit in a tube-shaped fuselage. The pilot and other crew sit on the flight deck at the front. The wings are roughly in the middle of the fuselage and are angled backwards. The tailfin ("tail") and tailplane (two small back wings) are clustered around the rear, which tapers to a point.

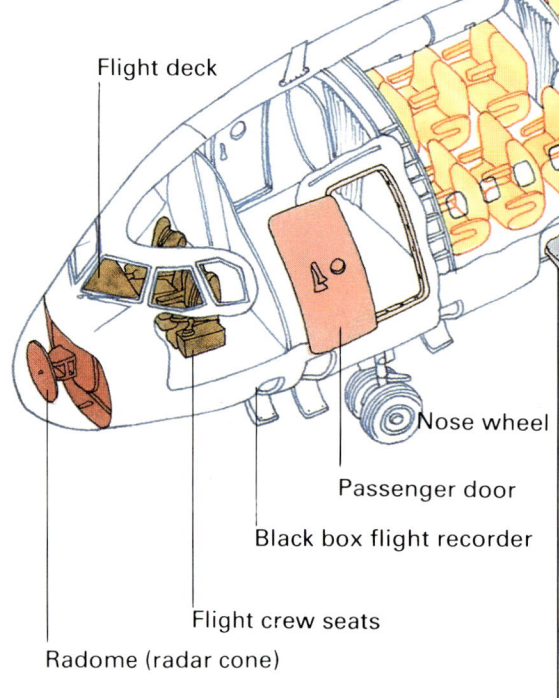

Flight deck

Cargo door

Nose wheel

First class passenger seats

Passenger door

Engine

Black box flight recorder

Flight crew seats

Radome (radar cone)

Pneumatic system

This works by pressurized air and controls the air conditioning, cabin pressurization, wing de-icing and many other processes. There are two independent systems, in case one fails.

Spoilers

Flaps

Slats

Hydraulic system

Pumps in the engines pressurize fluid which operates the flying control surfaces, cargo doors, landing gear and brakes. Three separate systems are used, in case of failure.

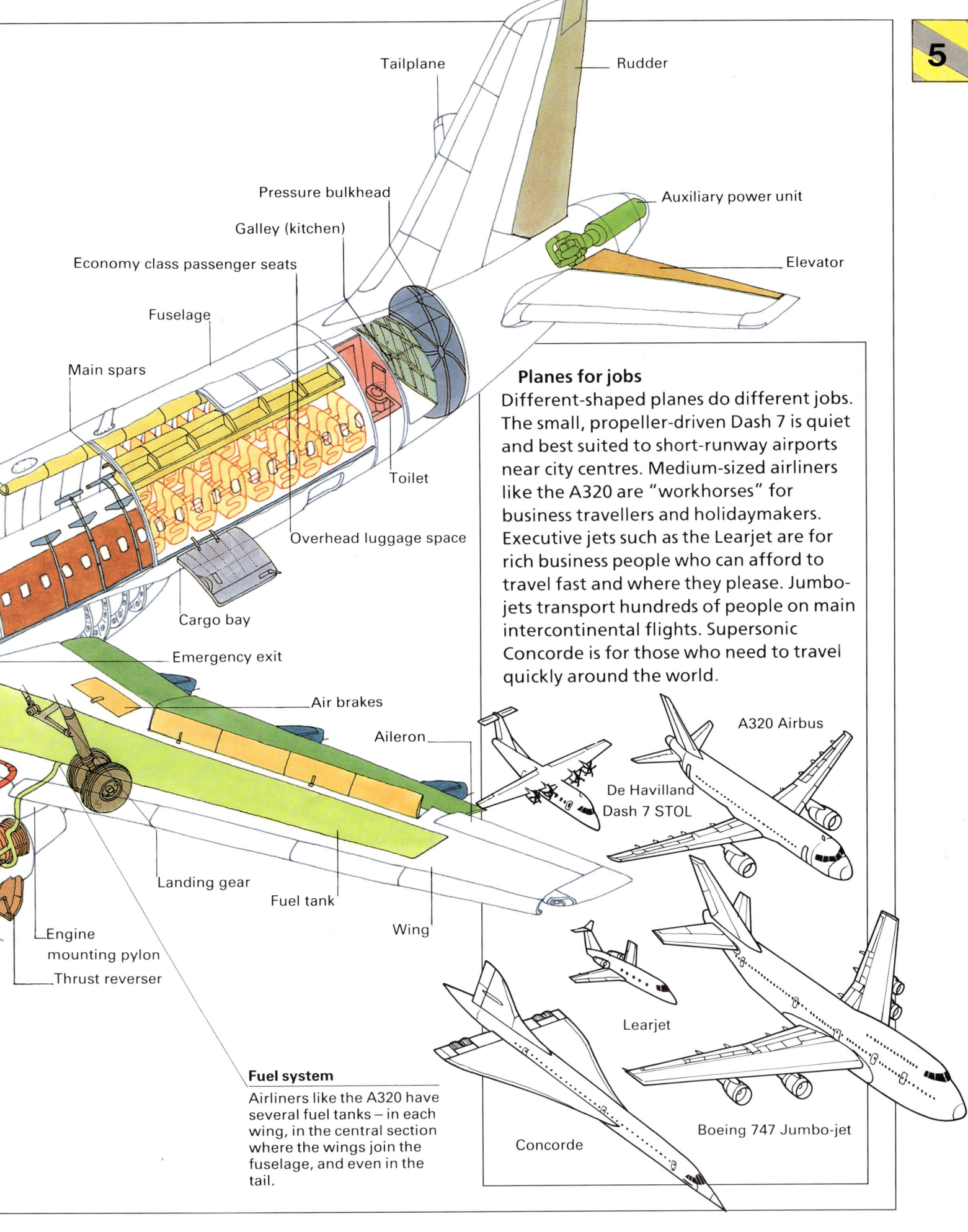

Tailplane

Rudder

Pressure bulkhead

Galley (kitchen)

Auxiliary power unit

Economy class passenger seats

Fuselage

Elevator

Main spars

Toilet

Overhead luggage space

Cargo bay

Emergency exit

Air brakes

Aileron

Landing gear

Fuel tank

Wing

Engine mounting pylon

Thrust reverser

Planes for jobs

Different-shaped planes do different jobs. The small, propeller-driven Dash 7 is quiet and best suited to short-runway airports near city centres. Medium-sized airliners like the A320 are "workhorses" for business travellers and holidaymakers. Executive jets such as the Learjet are for rich business people who can afford to travel fast and where they please. Jumbo-jets transport hundreds of people on main intercontinental flights. Supersonic Concorde is for those who need to travel quickly around the world.

A320 Airbus

De Havilland
Dash 7 STOL

Learjet

Boeing 747 Jumbo-jet

Concorde

Fuel system

Airliners like the A320 have several fuel tanks – in each wing, in the central section where the wings join the fuselage, and even in the tail.

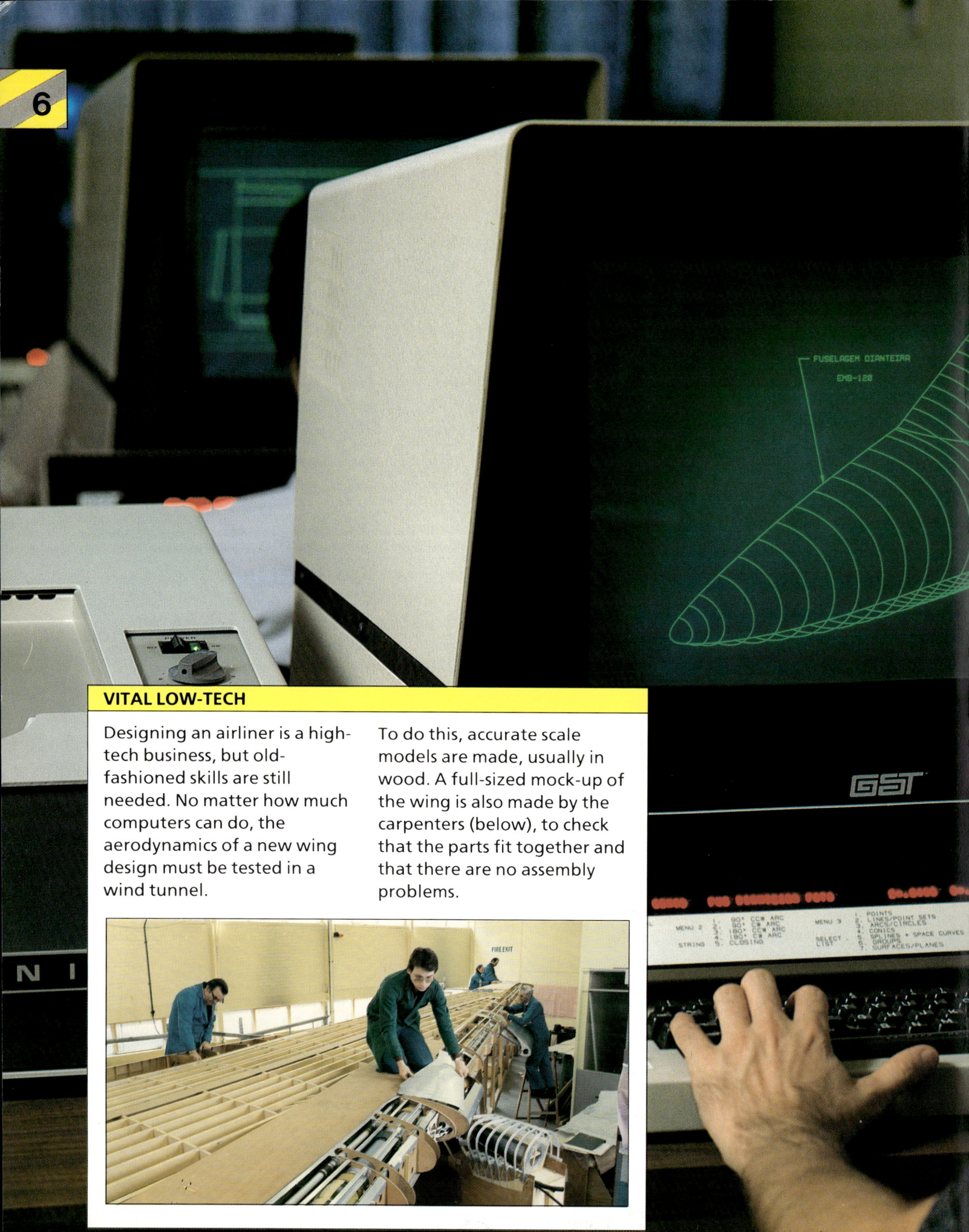

FUSELAGEM DIANTEIRA
EMB-120

GST

VITAL LOW-TECH

Designing an airliner is a high-tech business, but old-fashioned skills are still needed. No matter how much computers can do, the aerodynamics of a new wing design must be tested in a wind tunnel.

To do this, accurate scale models are made, usually in wood. A full-sized mock-up of the wing is also made by the carpenters (below), to check that the parts fit together and that there are no assembly problems.

FIRE EXIT

DESIGN

Apart from the supersonic Concorde, overall airplane design has changed little since the 1950s. So, when developing a new airliner, the designers and engineers do not have to go back to the basic principles of where to put the wings and engines. But there are new problems. For example, some manufacturers do not plan one type of plane. Just as cars come as a saloon model, a hatchback, an estate and a turbo version, so the modern plane may be designed as part of a "family". It can be made in a smaller version, or widened, or fitted with new engines, as the airlines require.

Nowadays, it is unlikely that every part of a plane will be made in the same factory, or even in the same town. Many different companies are involved. The main manufacturer may "subcontract" other companies in other cities to make specialized parts such as the radar equipment, seating, engines and hydraulic pumps. In the Airbus airliners this is taken even further: the fuselage is made in one country, the wings in another, the flight deck and tail in another.

NEW MATERIALS

Airplane designers are constantly searching for new metals, plastics and "composite" materials. These must be strong yet light, to help reduce weight and so save fuel. They must also be fully tested to make sure they can stand up to the stresses and strains of many hours in the air. In the Airbus A320, these lightweight materials are used extensively in the wings, brakes, engine mountings and covers, nose radar dome, landing gear doors, tailplane and tailfin. Using these new materials weight savings can be as much as one-quarter compared to all-metal components.

■ Composite materials

Computer-aided design

THE ENGINES

Engines are nearly always made by a separate manufacturer to the main airliner. The plane's engineers and designers are faced with a problem: should engines be used that are already in production, and tried and tested, or should they rely on the engine manufacturer to develop a new one, with perhaps more power at less cost?

In practice, airplane makers and engine makers spend a lot of time talking to each other. The engine manufacturers know the sort of engines that are likely to be in demand, and which types of engines their competitors are planning. The plane makers know which sorts of engines are under development, and they will talk to the various engine makers, such as Rolls Royce and Pratt & Whitney, with the aim of getting the best deal.

To save the costs of developing a completely new engine, the engine designers may try to "stretch" one of their current versions, in the way that a car engine can be made more powerful by using fuel injection or turbocharge.

The modern turbofan is the powerhouse of most of today's airliners. At full power it can swallow a tonne of air every second.

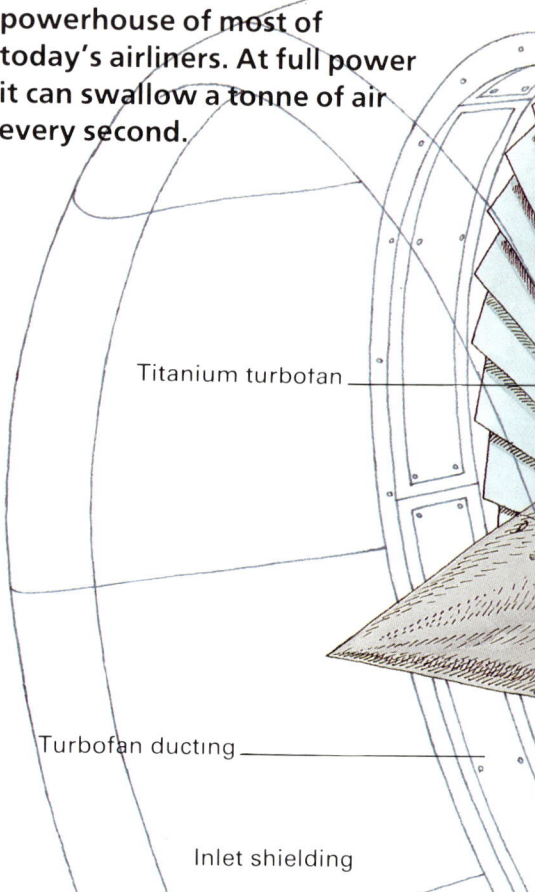

Titanium turbofan

Turbofan ducting

Inlet shielding

TYPES OF JET ENGINES

There are three main types of jet engines. In the turbojet, air is sucked through the inlet (1) into the compressor (2). This is driven by the engine's main shaft (3). Hot compressed air enters the combustion chamber (4) where it is mixed with fuel and ignited. The expanding gases drive the turbine (5) and rush out of the back as the exhaust jet (6), which pushes the plane forward. The more common turbofan has many parts similar to those of the turbojet. An extra turbine (7), connected to an inner shaft (8), drives a big fan (9) at the front of the engine. This blows huge quantities of air through a duct (10) around the engine, which gives extra thrust for the same amount of fuel. The turboprop is similar to the turbojet, but a propeller (11) blows air around the engine rather than through a duct.

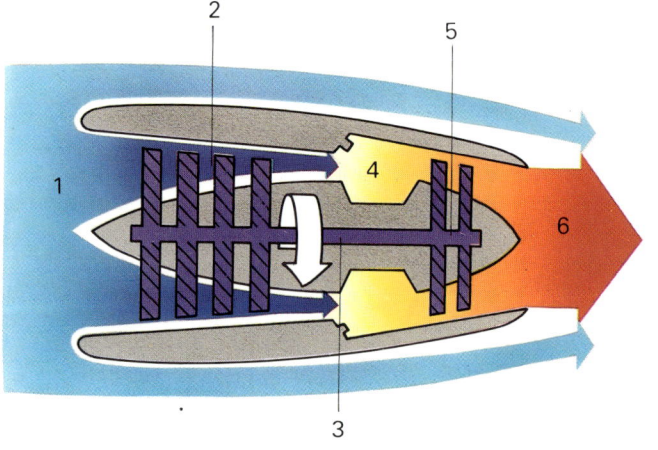

Turbojet

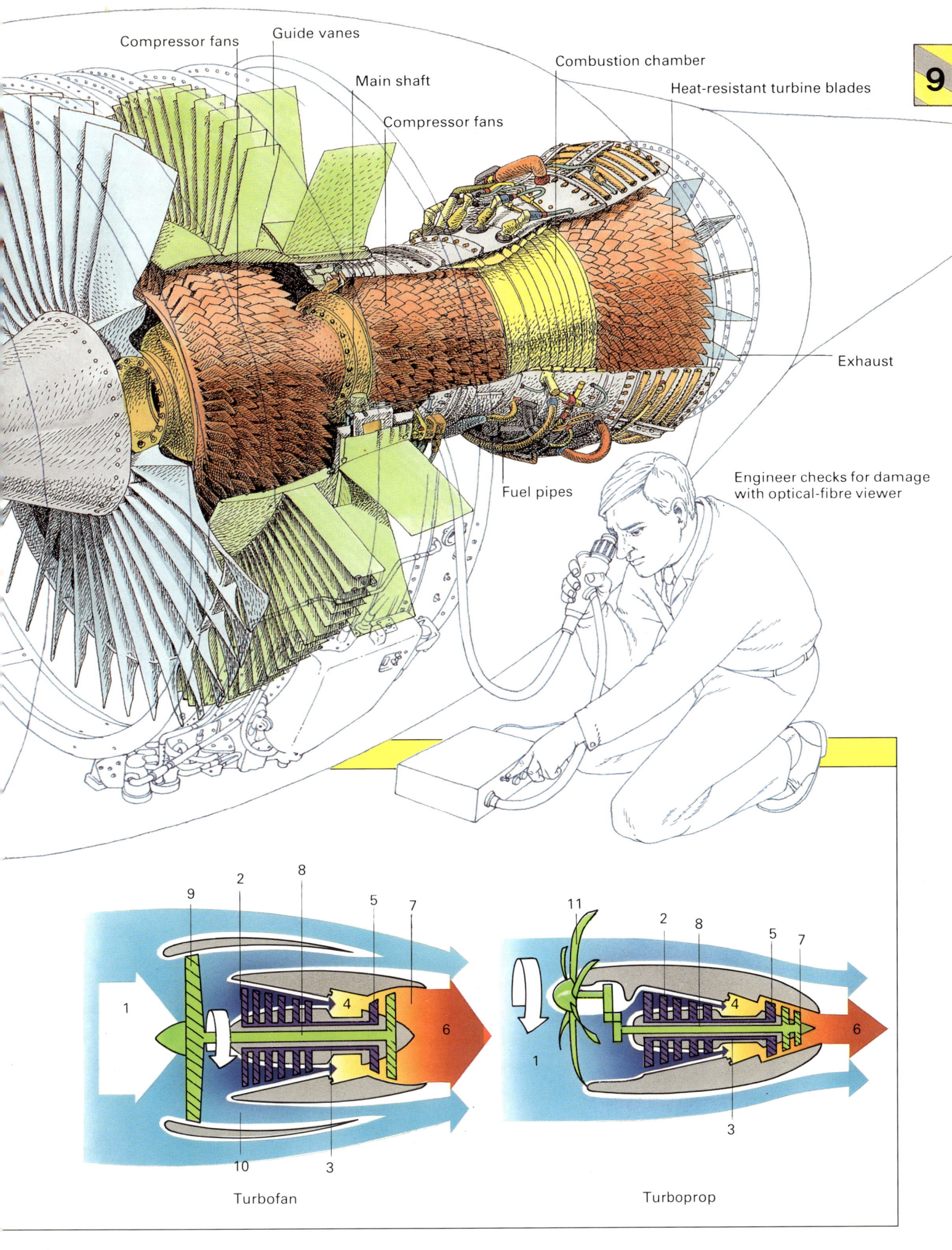

Compressor fans

Guide vanes

Main shaft

Compressor fans

Combustion chamber

Heat-resistant turbine blades

Exhaust

Fuel pipes

Engineer checks for damage with optical-fibre viewer

Turbofan

Turboprop

ON THE TEST BED

During its lifetime a passenger airliner will carry millions of people, and fly over towns and cities. So it is vital that every part is tested thoroughly. Each component is tested under normal conditions, to make sure that it works as it was designed to. It is then tested to extremes. The mechanisms inside the wings are subjected to sub-zero temperatures, and then hot sand is shovelled into them – since the same plane has to work in polar areas and in tropical deserts. Dead chickens are thrown into the engines, to make sure they still work if birds are accidentally sucked into them.

Then each part is tested to destruction. The engines roar at full power until they break down. The wings are bent until they snap. The cause of failure is found, and it must be as predicted by the designer. Other tests copy the stresses caused by take-off and landing. These tests continue as long as the plane is flying, so that the parts under test have done at least two-and-a-half times as many "flights" as any plane in service.

Computers predict how a new design will perform. Even so, a model is tested in a wind tunnel, to detect any problems before full-sized parts are made.

The wings of a modern airliner have a certain amount of flexibility built in. They are able to absorb the bumps of landings and air turbulence, by bending.

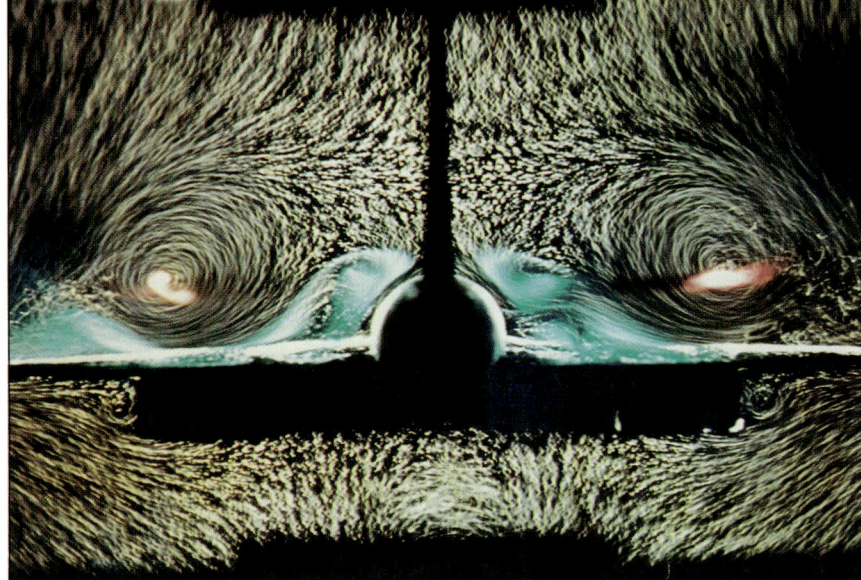

WAGGLING THE WINGS

Wires attached to the wings bend them by a measured amount along their lengths.

Pressure is slowly applied until they snap, usually at an angle of 30 degrees.

BUILDING THE PARTS

Many thousands of components, from main wing spars to tiny light bulbs, go to make up today's airliner. Smaller parts may be made by many different companies, often in different places. So they are often pre-assembled into larger units called "modules". Some manufacturers bring together the modules on their main production line. Others gather groups of modules and connect them into

This central section of an Airbus A320 fuselage has plugs, sockets and joints at each end. On the production line, it can be "plugged in" to the others, so that the wires, pipes and cables connect up.

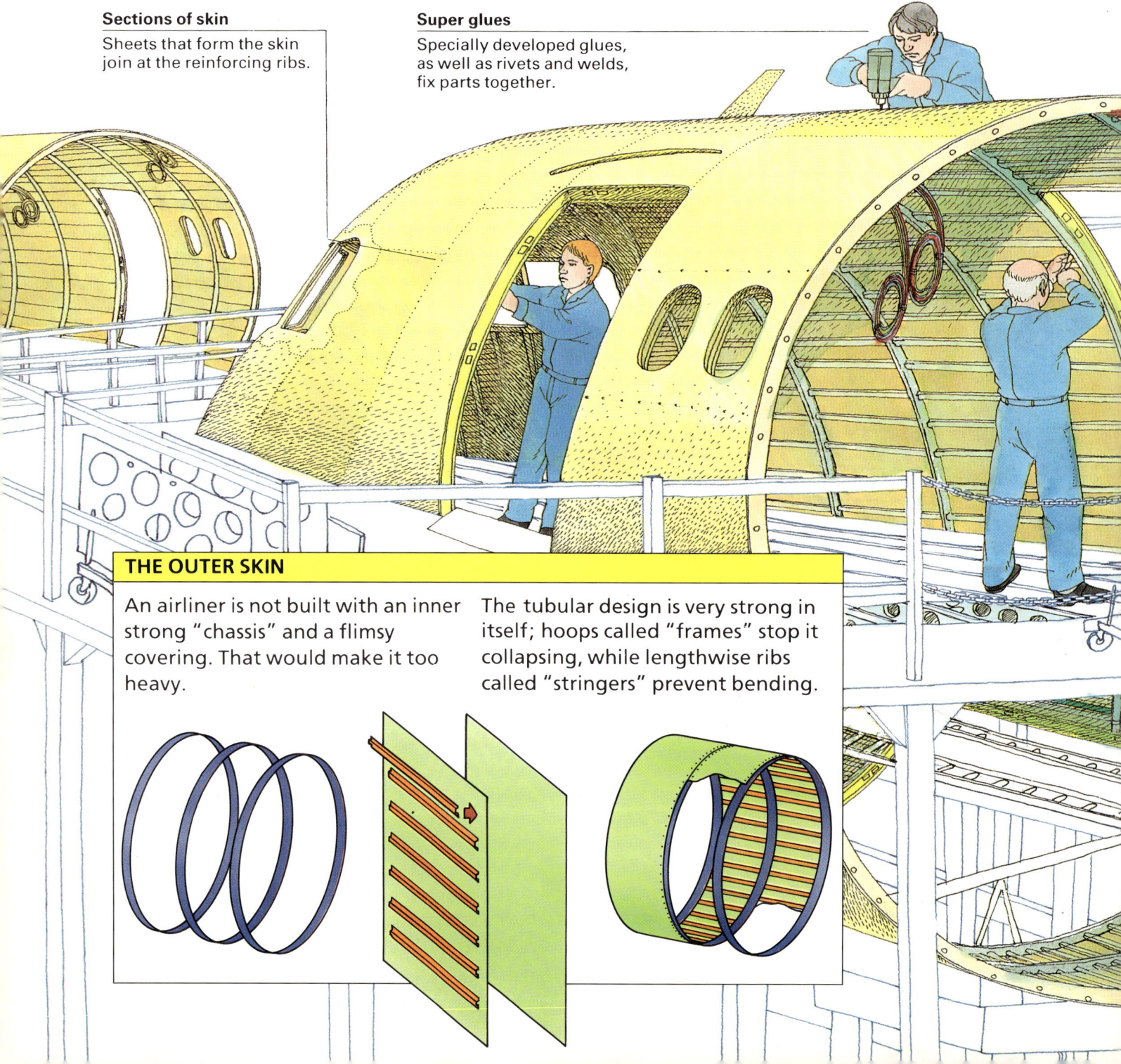

Sections of skin

Sheets that form the skin join at the reinforcing ribs.

Super glues

Specially developed glues, as well as rivets and welds, fix parts together.

THE OUTER SKIN

An airliner is not built with an inner strong "chassis" and a flimsy covering. That would make it too heavy.

The tubular design is very strong in itself; hoops called "frames" stop it collapsing, while lengthwise ribs called "stringers" prevent bending.

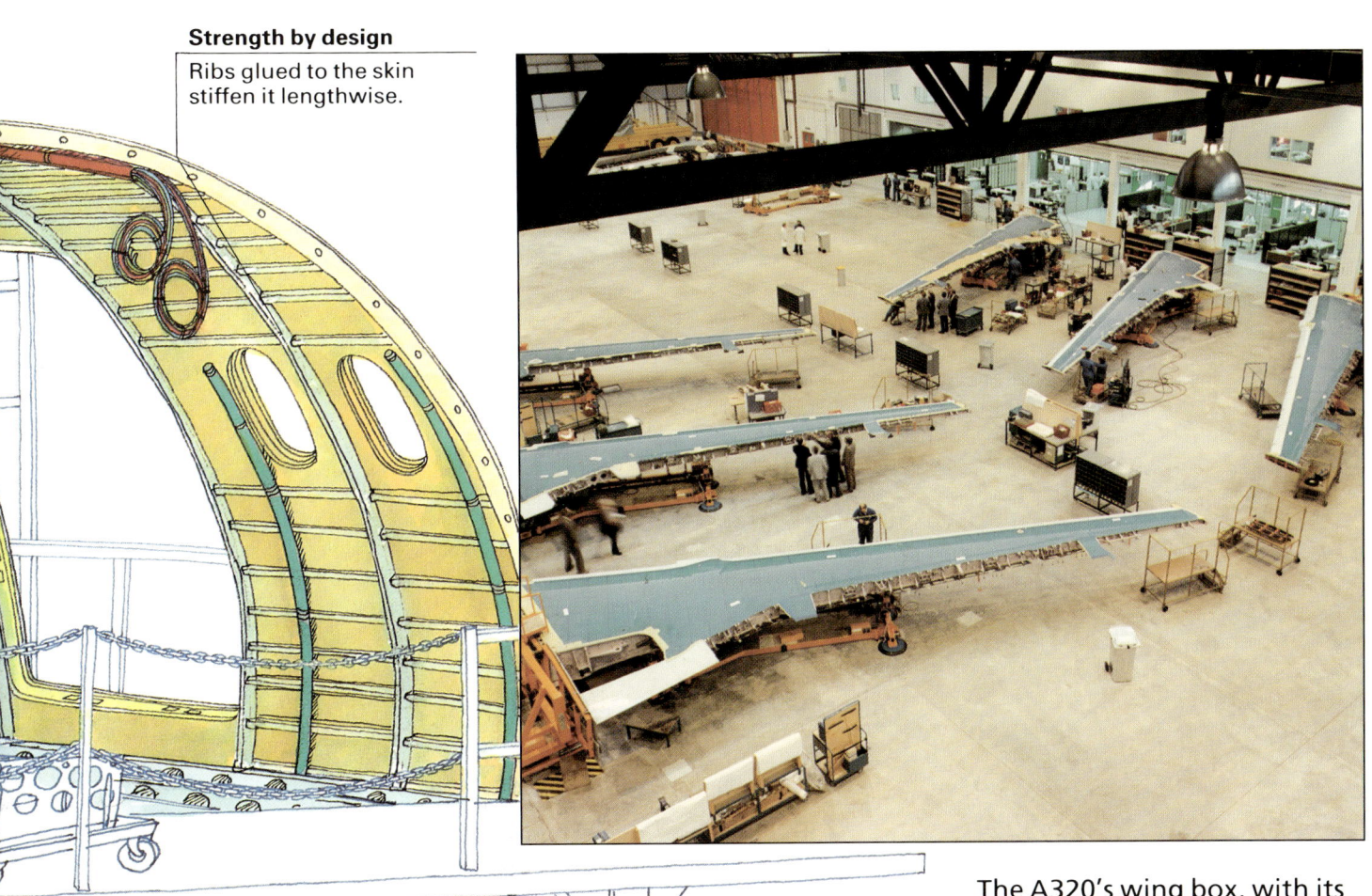

larger sections, often called "assemblies", such as a wing or fuselage. Assemblies are then taken to the main production line.

The engineers and fitters must plan the order of work exactly, so that parts are installed before the section is covered or sealed in. For example, the outer wall or "skin" of the fuselage may be made from flat sheets of aluminium alloy. Stiffening ribs are glued lengthwise to it, then it is bent around circular strengthening hoops. Holes are cut in the skin for doors and windows. All the cables and pipes that run through the fuselage must be laid in place, before the inner floor and walls are installed.

Strength by design

Ribs glued to the skin stiffen it lengthwise.

Electrics

Wires that run through the fuselage are laid as it is being built.

Hydraulics

Empty lengths of pipe will become the hydraulic system. After final assembly the fluids are put into the pipes and pressurized.

The A320's wing box, with its internal fuel tanks, is fitted with the tracks that carry the flaps. The hydraulic and mechanical systems that control the flaps are installed. Slats, ailerons and flaps are added, and the whole assembly is tested to make sure it works.

INSTALLING SYSTEMS

Although the basic design of an airliner has not changed much over the years, the insides certainly have. Development engineers are producing smaller and lighter electric motors, switches and hydraulic pumps, to replace the old steel cables, levers and rods. The changes are particularly noticeable on the flight deck, the "brain of the plane". In the Airbus A320, for example, the engineers have developed a "fly-by-wire" system. Gone is the large,

The flight deck is the nerve centre of the airliner. From here, both pilot and co-pilot have full control. They can see at a glance the height, speed and direction of flight, the condition of the engines and various systems, fuel reserves and engine economy, and even the temperature and other conditions in the passenger cabin.

FLY-BY-WIRE

The Airbus A320 makes full use of "fly-by-wire". Heavy cables and pipes that ran between the flight deck and the various moving parts have been replaced by light electrical wires. The main control is a small computer-type joystick. The computer "reads" the stick's movements and sends signals to actuators (electric motors and hydraulic pumps) which move the various control surfaces.

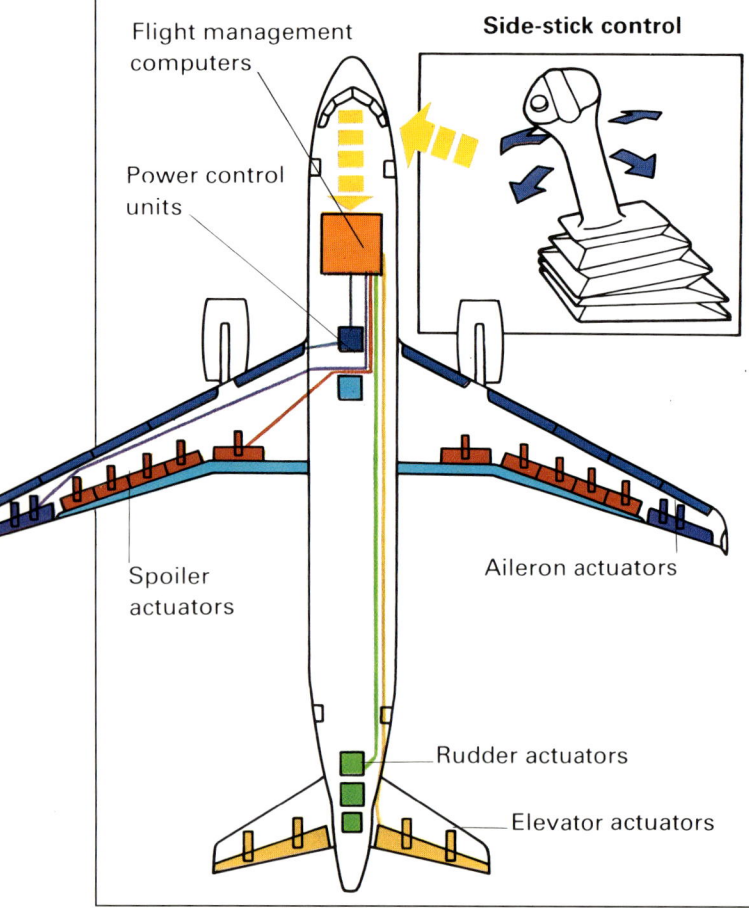

Flight management computers

Power control units

Side-stick control

Spoiler actuators

Aileron actuators

Rudder actuators

Elevator actuators

central control column. In its place is a small side-stick. This is similar to the joysticks used in computer controls. Everything in the plane can now be controlled electrically from the flight deck, with great savings in weight and less chance of mechanical failure.

In modern airliners, the rows of dials and winking lights are gradually being replaced by small computer screens. These display flight and navigational information, all in one place and at the touch of a button. They also give readouts of fuel consumption, engine performance and any malfunctions.

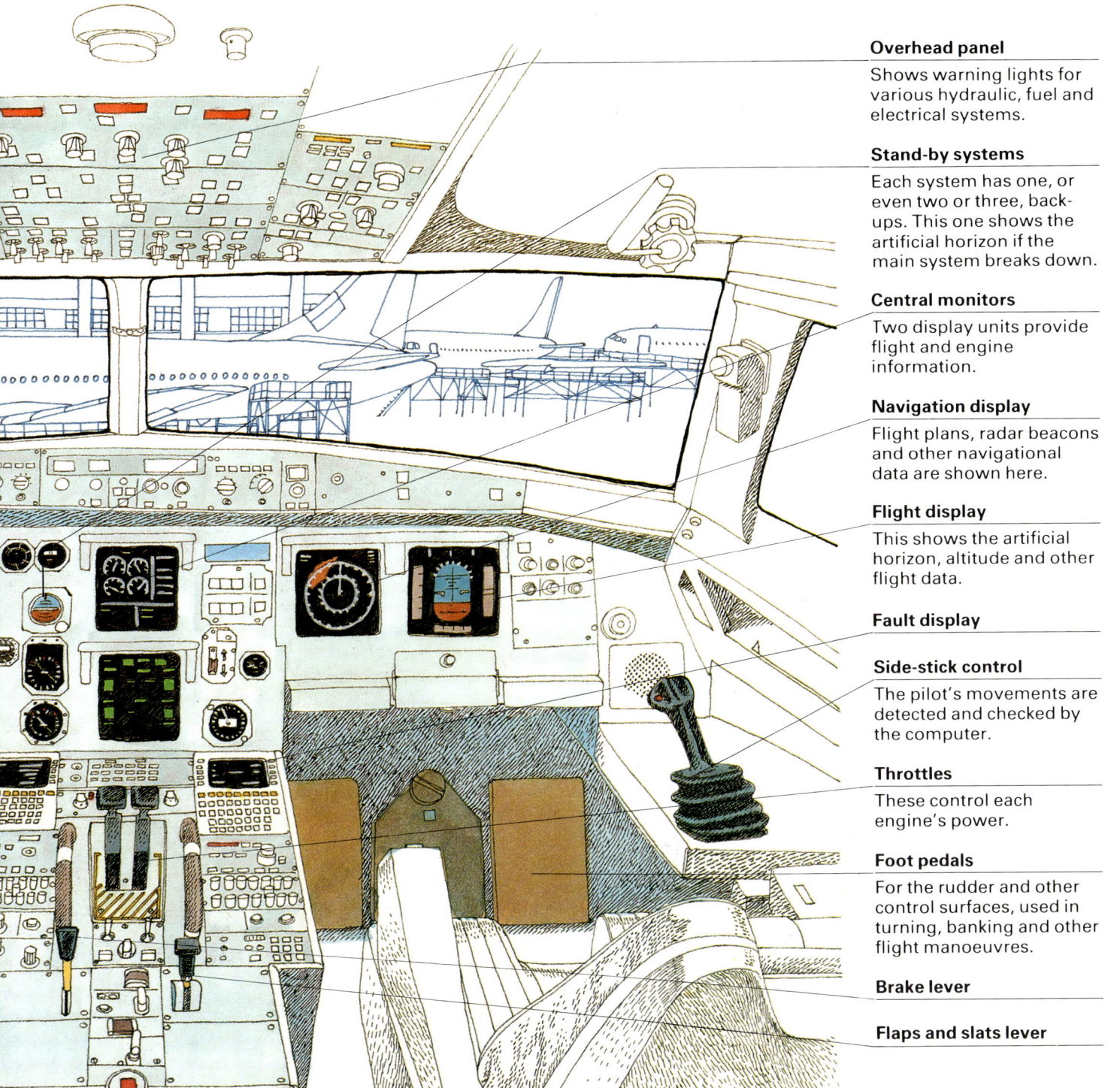

Overhead panel

Shows warning lights for various hydraulic, fuel and electrical systems.

Stand-by systems

Each system has one, or even two or three, back-ups. This one shows the artificial horizon if the main system breaks down.

Central monitors

Two display units provide flight and engine information.

Navigation display

Flight plans, radar beacons and other navigational data are shown here.

Flight display

This shows the artificial horizon, altitude and other flight data.

Fault display

Side-stick control

The pilot's movements are detected and checked by the computer.

Throttles

These control each engine's power.

Foot pedals

For the rudder and other control surfaces, used in turning, banking and other flight manoeuvres.

Brake lever

Flaps and slats lever

Fuselage

The main body of the fuselage is joined to the the cockpit and tail sections. They are riveted together to complete fuselage assembly.

Wings

The intricate fuel, pneumatic, hydraulic and electrical systems to the engines and flaps are linked.

Tail

As the upright tailfin and the two small wings of the tailplane are added, the plane takes its final shape. Again the control systems are connected at the joins.

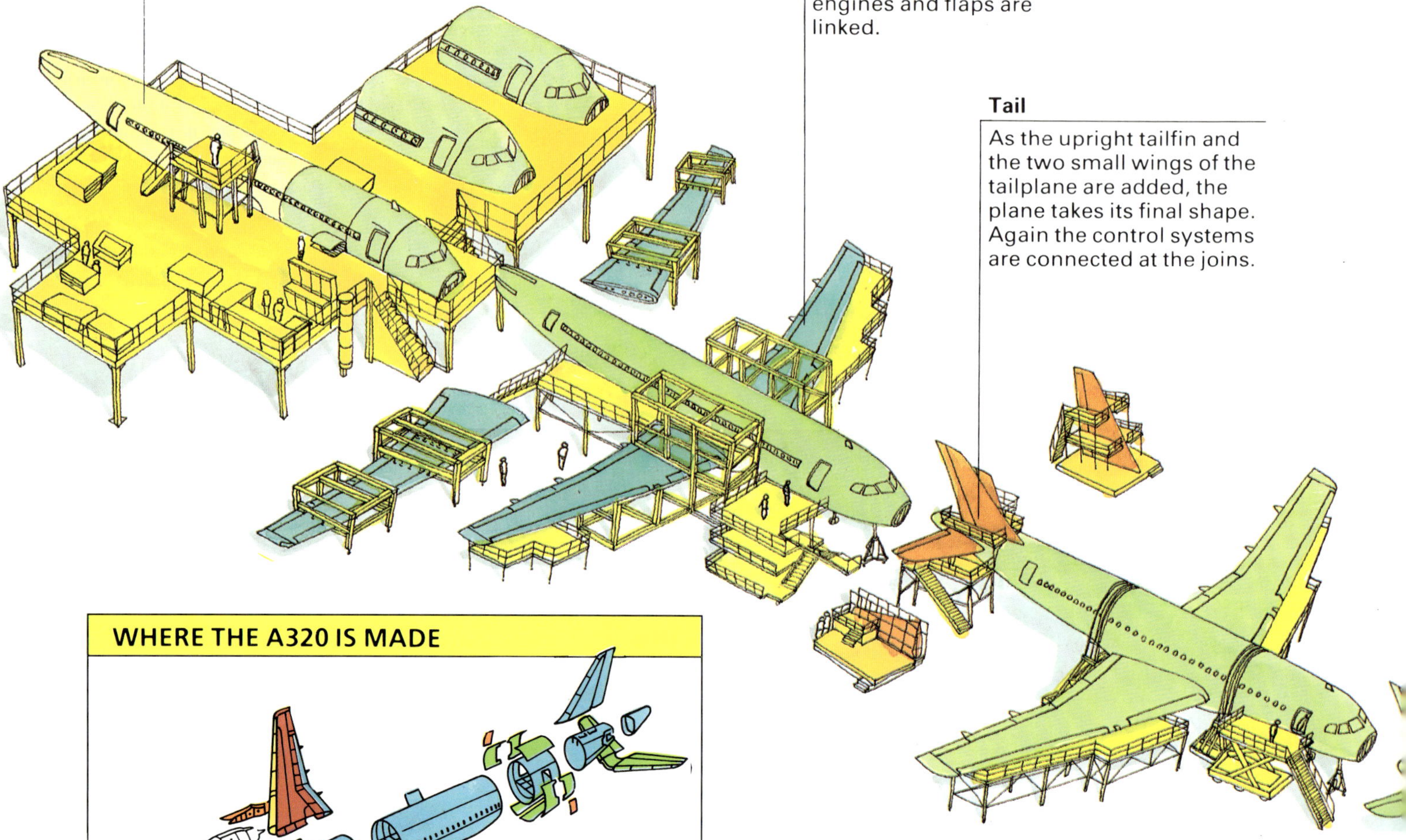

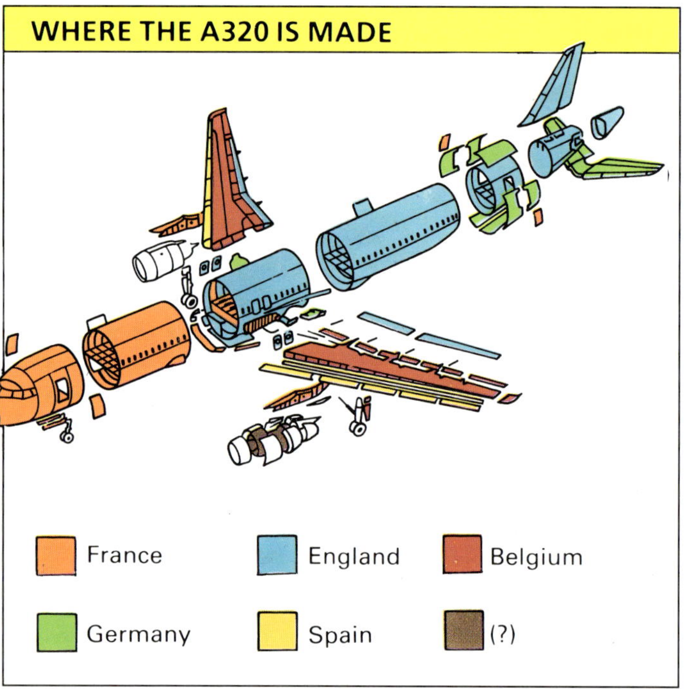

WHERE THE A320 IS MADE

■ France	■ England	■ Belgium
■ Germany	■ Spain	■ (?)

Airbus Industries is a group of European companies. Each makes a section of A320 airliner in its own country (left). A specially enlarged plane, the Guppy, transports the sections to the main production line in Toulouse, France.

When each part of the plane has been made and tested it is brought to the main production line. Piece by piece the finished airliner takes shape, like an enormous jigsaw, as the parts are joined and the systems connected.

In the old days, small airplane manufacturers would make one plane at a time. They could not begin the next one until the first had been finished and towed away. Nowadays, building an airliner is much like building any other multi-part machine, such as a car. Several planes are made at once, on a production line housed in a giant hangar. In some cases the planes stay still and gangs of fitters and engineers move from one to the next. In other cases the plane moves from one specialized fitting bay to the next. The building with the largest volume in the world is Boeing's main assembly hangar at Everett, near Seattle, USA. Its volume is 5.6 million cubic metres.

The production line solves several problems. The workers become very skilled at doing their particular job, rather than having to tackle all the construction tasks — which in a modern airliner run into thousands. Also, valuable assembly machines and testing equipment are kept occupied, rather than lying idle as they wait for the next plane.

Pylons

The pylons carry controls to the engines, and they also take hydraulic, electrical and pneumatic power generated in the engines back to the wings and fuselage.

Engines

The engines are usually last on the line. The engine and plane manufacturers have worked closely together, so that there should be no problems fitting engines to pylons.

Systems testing

Once all the plane's control systems have been linked up, thorough checks are performed and problems ironed out. The radar dome on the plane's nose is fitted.

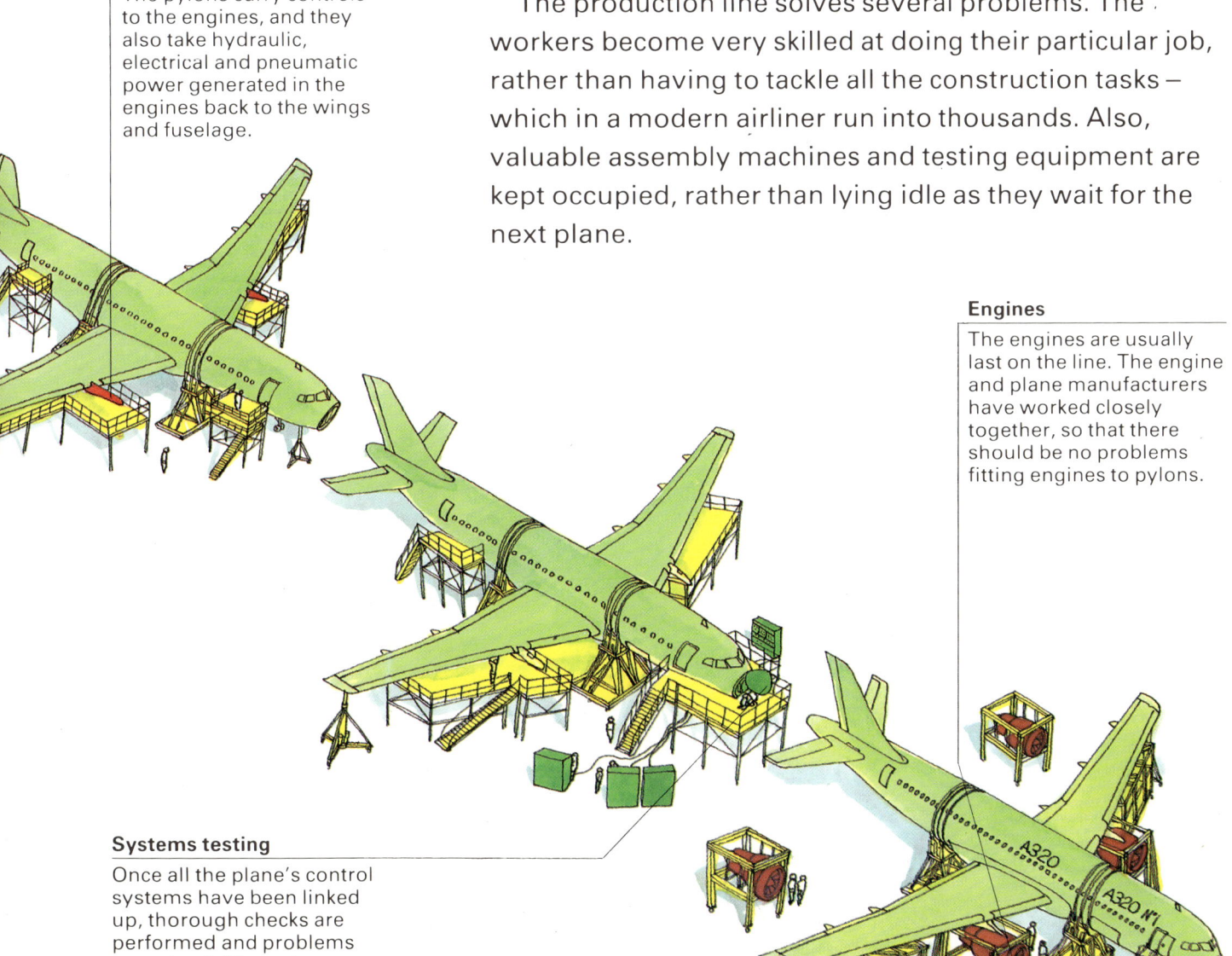

ROLL-OUT!

The "roll-out" of a new airliner is like the launch of a ship. For a short while, engineering considerations are put aside, and publicity is the name of the game. The researchers, designers and builders take a back seat as the sales team take over. The prototypes will be under construction, and many orders for future planes taken, but there is still more selling to do if the plane is to make a profit.

At the roll-out, the general public have their first chance to see the new plane "in the flesh". It is christened by important people, reported on in the newspapers and on television, and there are celebrations and much champagne is drunk.

The roll-out is the end of one phase, and the start of another. Engineers must now talk technicalities with airline representatives, about how the plane will perform and how it can be adapted to their needs. The plane on display is probably empty of seats and full of test equipment. It has never even flown – it still has to be put through its paces in the air.

Airliners carry cargo as well as people – the passengers' luggage, mail and other goods. On some routes passenger space may be occupied by cargo.

Passengers and luggage

Passengers, luggage and cargo

Cargo only

Roll-outs attract great attention from radio, television and newspapers thus helping the sales of a new airliner. The first one off the production line is "rolled out" in front of an invited crowd of photographers and reporters, sometimes with impressive gimmicks such as dry ice and laser lighting, as was the A320 in 1986 (right). The ability to vary the airliner's role is also a great selling point as is demonstrated in the pictures below showing the Boeing 757 rolled out as a passenger airliner (bottom left) and as a "Package Freighter" (bottom right). Producing the same basic airframe in a number of different guises helps to keep down the manufacturing costs.

WATFORD GRAMMAR SCHOOL
FULLER MEMORIAL.
LIBRARY

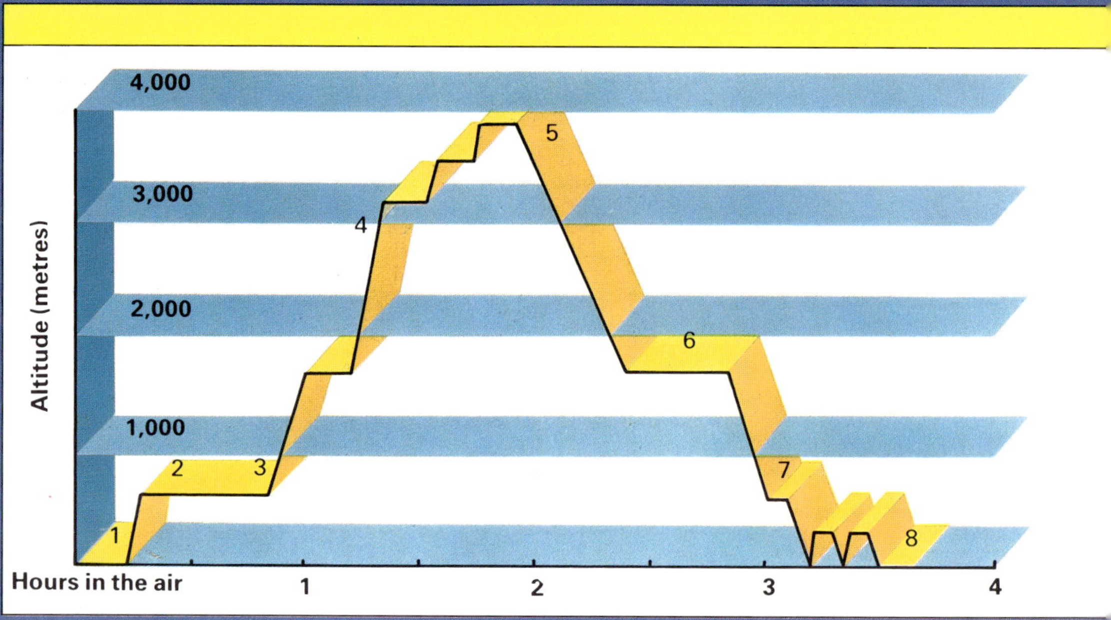
4,000
3,000
2,000
1,000
Altitude (metres)
Hours in the air
1
2
3
4
1
2
3
4
5
6
7
8

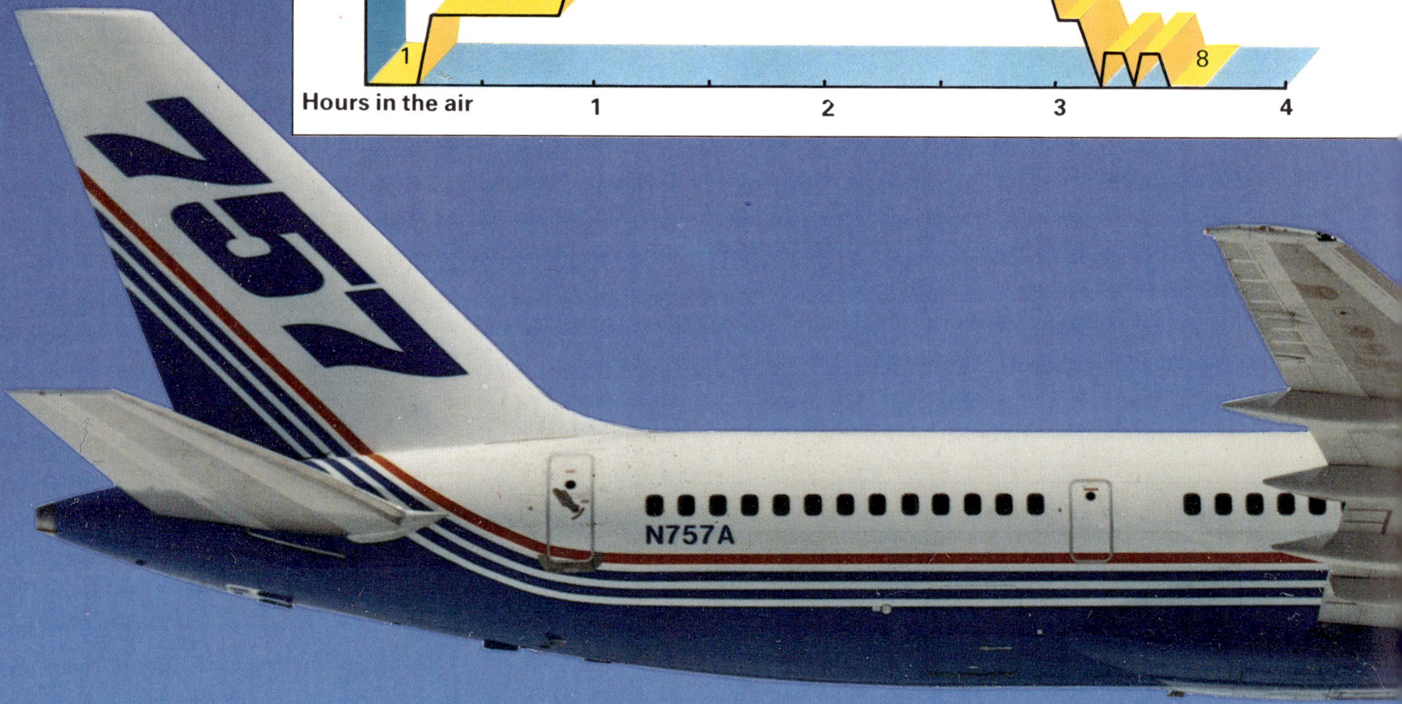
757
N757A

767
BOEING 767

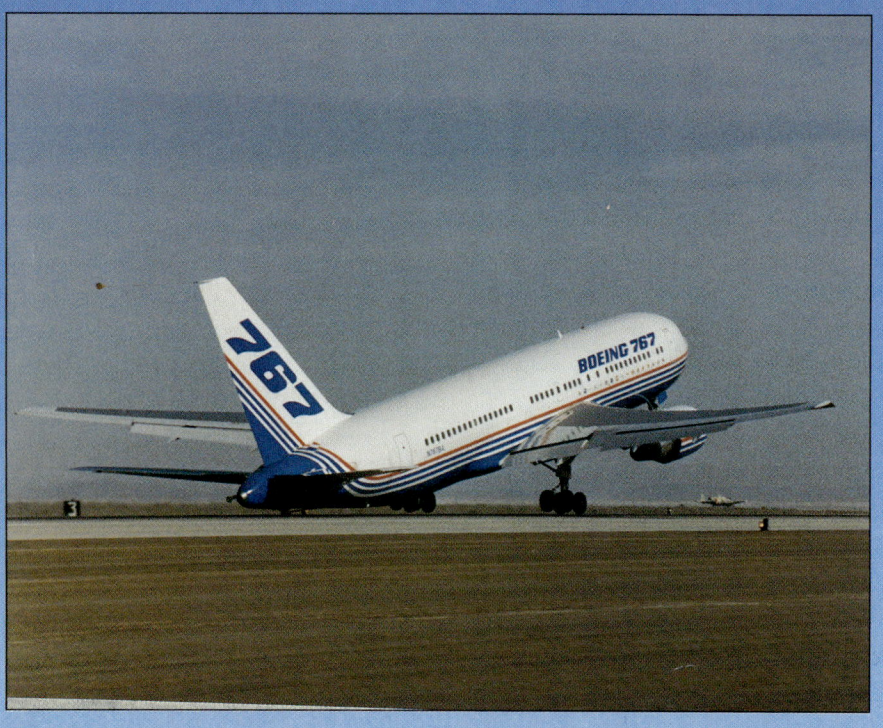

Take-off and landing are testing times for any plane. A new airliner must be able to lift off with its tail skid dragging along the ground, like the Boeing 767 on the left. It must also be able to brake to a halt even when the runway is flooded. These tests are carried out with the airliner loaded to its maximum operating weight, and in high and low temperatures.

TEST FLIGHT PROFILE

A typical test flight might begin with a check of flight controls (1), then rudder, ailerons and elevators (2), slats (3), autopilot (4), cabin depressurization and back to pilot control (5), airbrakes (6), landing navigation equipment (7), and a series of "touch-and-go" circuits to simulate emergency conditions. Finally the plane lands under autopilot control (8).

The engineers of today do not have one of the problems they would have faced 50 or 60 years ago: will it fly? Computers and calculations predict how the airliner should handle, long before it leaves the ground. But the test flight is still part of proving the plane. The first prototypes must be put through their paces in the air, to reveal any unexpected problems. If a limited redesign is necessary, the engineers must do this quickly so that planes on the main production line can be modified before full production begins. This is why there is a gap, often of many months, between the test flight and the airliner entering service.

The first prototypes are packed with complicated test equipment. The test pilots take them through a series of turns, climbs and dives at various heights, to see if they perform as expected. Here a Boeing 757 is put through its paces. Other planes fly alongside to check the outside condition and to take photographs for technical examination (and for publicity!).

A new airliner must receive a certificate of airworthiness before it can carry passengers. The process of getting this certificate does not begin with the test flight, however. The authorities monitor the building of every part of the plane. Engineering standards, manufacturing processes, the materials used and the design are all checked. Once in the air, the test pilots have to get the "feel" of a plane that no one has ever flown before. They must rigorously check how it handles at different heights and different speeds, and that it can cope with emergencies such as an engine failure.

SAFETY FIRST

Airliner engineers keep to the highest standards possible. There is no room for failure when 400 people are travelling at 250 metres per second, 10 kilometres up. If something does go wrong, an airliner must contain safety features which help to save lives.

On the ground, a fire in the passenger cabin can cause choking smoke and intense heat. It must be possible to evacuate all the passengers in 90 seconds, with the use of emergency chutes. Seat belts must be provided, for comfort as well as safety. Each passenger must have an oxygen supply, in case the cabin loses its pressurization and the air becomes too thin to breathe. On flights over water, there must be a life-jacket under every seat.

Every time there is a crash, investigators are soon on the scene to find the cause. Other planes are checked to make sure that a similar accident could not happen again. New regulations and safety procedures may be brought in. Everything humanly possible is done to keep flying as the safest form of travel.

Safety signs
Illuminated signs at the front of each compartment tell the passengers when they can smoke and when to put on their seat belts. Smoking is not allowed during take-off and landing.

Oxygen masks
If the cabin air leaks out, the passengers must be given oxygen to breathe. Oxygen masks automatically fall from the racks above each seat.

Life-jackets

These are stored under the seats. They fit over the head and tie around the waist. They self-inflate when the wearer pulls a toggle. Before a flight over water, the cabin crew are required to show all passengers how to put on the life-jacket and operate the toggle, light and whistle.

Seat belts
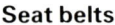
Every seat has a seat belt that clips around the person's waist. This has to be fastened for take-off and landing and if the plane hits air turbulence.

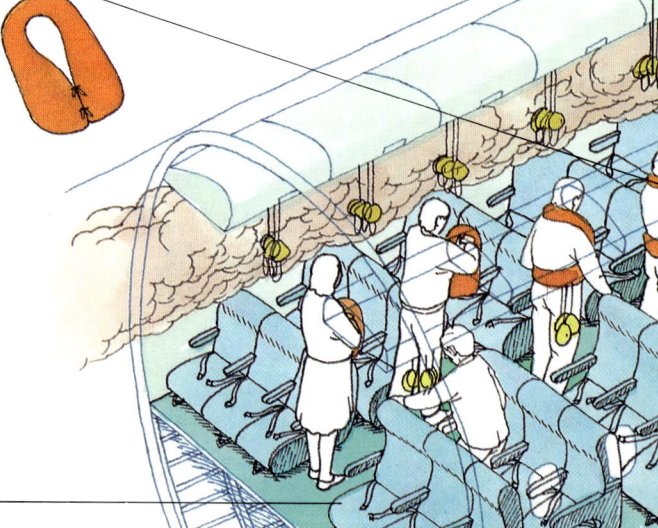

PREVENTING A FIREBALL

If a plane crashes, the mixture of air and fuel vapour in its tanks can explode like a bomb. This test for a safer fuel in 1985, using an old remote-controlled plane, did not work. Now scientists have found a way to join the molecules of fuel into long chains which do not easily vapourize. Between the fuel tanks and the engine is a converter which chops up the long molecules again so that it can be burnt as fuel in the engines.

Airliners must meet certain safety standards before they can go into service. Shown here are some of the major safety features.

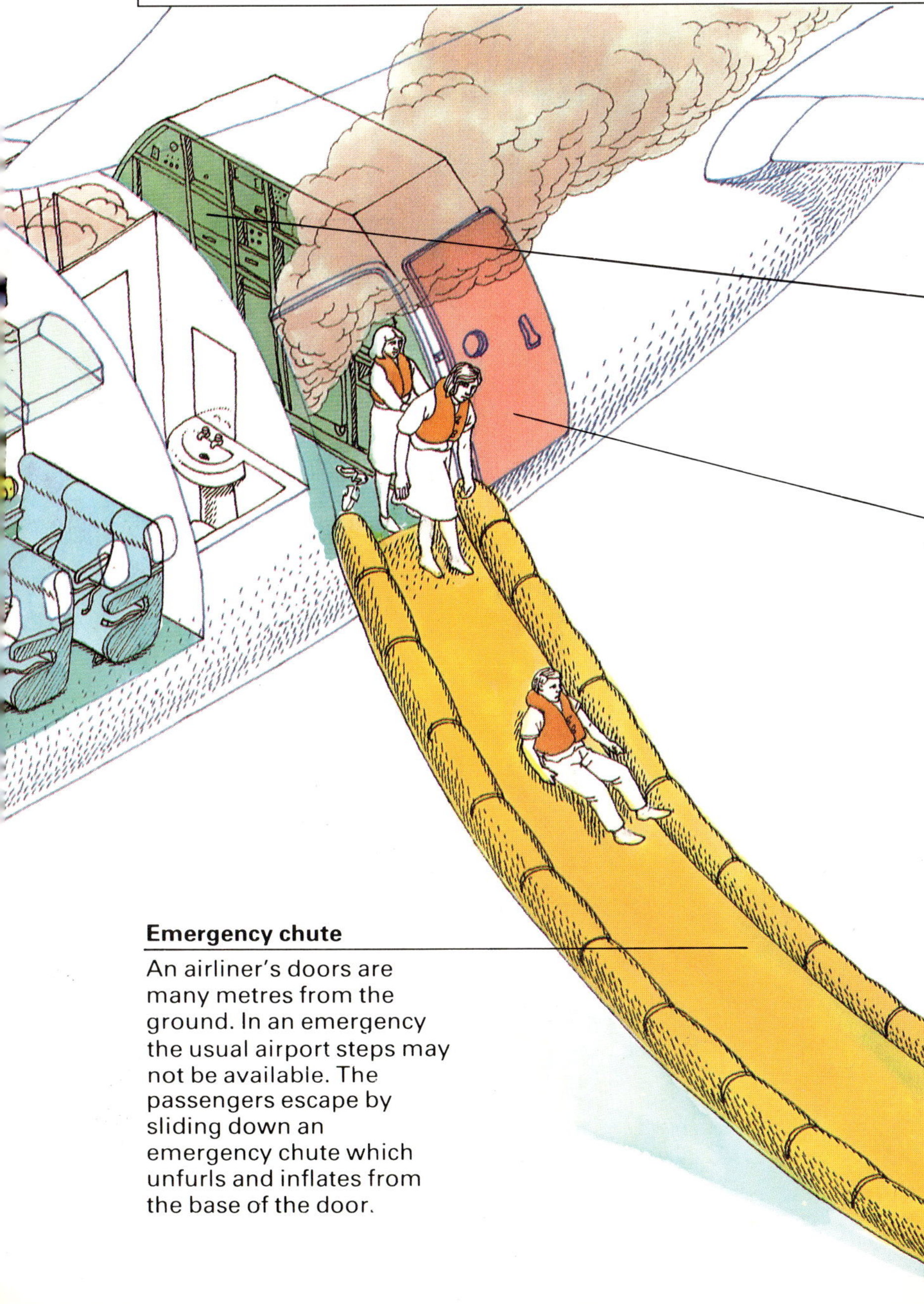

Safe storage

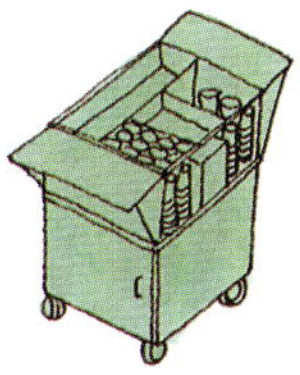

Cabin contents such as meal trays are stored in closed cupboards so that they are not thrown around the cabin in an emergency.

Emergency exits

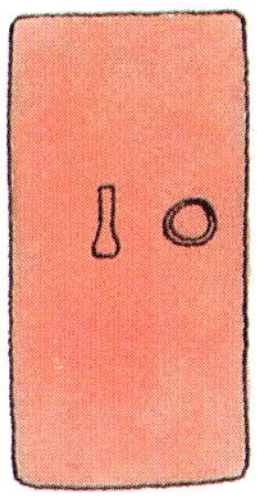

In the event of a crash, passengers must be able to get out of the plane quickly. As well as the regular doors, there are emergency doors over the wings and at the back.

Emergency chute

An airliner's doors are many metres from the ground. In an emergency the usual airport steps may not be available. The passengers escape by sliding down an emergency chute which unfurls and inflates from the base of the door.

INTO SERVICE

Designing and building an airliner is only part of the engineer's task. Once in service, it must be maintained in complete working order. This means devising a service schedule according to which parts of the plane need checking, and when, and how long this will take. Most modern airliners run "on condition". If a part is working well, it is left. If there is any sign that something is wrong, it is replaced. Normally each engine has to be removed for a refit after 3,000 to 5,000 hours of running time. This is about once a year for an average airliner. Tyres may be replaced every 100 or so landings. More complex checks occur at scheduled intervals. For example, the insides of the fuel tanks are inspected only every five years or so.

After an airliner lands it has to be refuelled and quickly prepared for its next flight. It is designed so that the various service trucks can come alongside all at once. These begin their work even before the passenger doors are opened. Within 30 minutes all the turn-around tasks will be complete and the airliner will be taxiing back to the runway.

Finishing touches: An Airbus receives its airline's colours.

Such rigorous attention to safety at each stop-over does not normally delay the plane. Ground engineers examine key parts while the service trucks come alongside to load and unload. It takes around 30 minutes to replace almost any serviced part, while an average turn-around time from engine shutdown to restart is 35 minutes. On a normal stop, refuelling takes up most of the time.

Galley service vehicle
brings trays of food and drink and removes old ones

Ground electrical power vehicle
supplies electricity while engines are shut down

Water service vehicle

Towing tractor

IN FOR A SERVICE

This A300 Airbus of Lufthansa Airlines is undergoing a routine inspection in one of the airline's servicing bays. Worn or faulty parts are replaced. Minor services occur almost weekly; major ones after a few months. Airliners are built today so that faulty parts can be replaced quickly and efficiently.

Bulk cargo loader
with crates, baggage and parcels

Container loader
transports prepacked standard-sized containers of air freight

Toilet service vehicle
empties toilet and basin wastes and supplies disinfectant flushing fluids

Air conditioning vehicle
maintains cabin conditions while plane's system is switched off

"Jetway"
walkways extend from the airport building straight to the door

Passenger stairs vehicle

THE YOUNG ENGINEER

Airliners are some of the most complicated machines ever made. The modern jetliner is a far cry from the propeller-driven biplane passenger plane of 50 years ago. Yet they both use the same simple engineering principles. Try the projects shown here, which demonstrate some of the basic scientific laws involved in building and flying a plane.

The compressor
Modern jet engines rely on the simple principle of compressing air. The air is taken in through a large-diameter intake. This narrows to a smaller diameter. Incoming air presses on the air already in the engine which, as it passes into the narrower space, is squeezed and speeds up. You can demonstrate this using a hair-dryer set on "cold". Try to blow out a candle at the distance of one or two metres (1). The air from the nozzle spreads out and is unlikely to extinguish the flame. Place a funnel shape over the nozzle (2). This compresses and concentrates the air into a narrower, faster stream that should blow out the candle. The large intake and small exhaust of a jet engine (3) work in the same way (as explained on page 8).

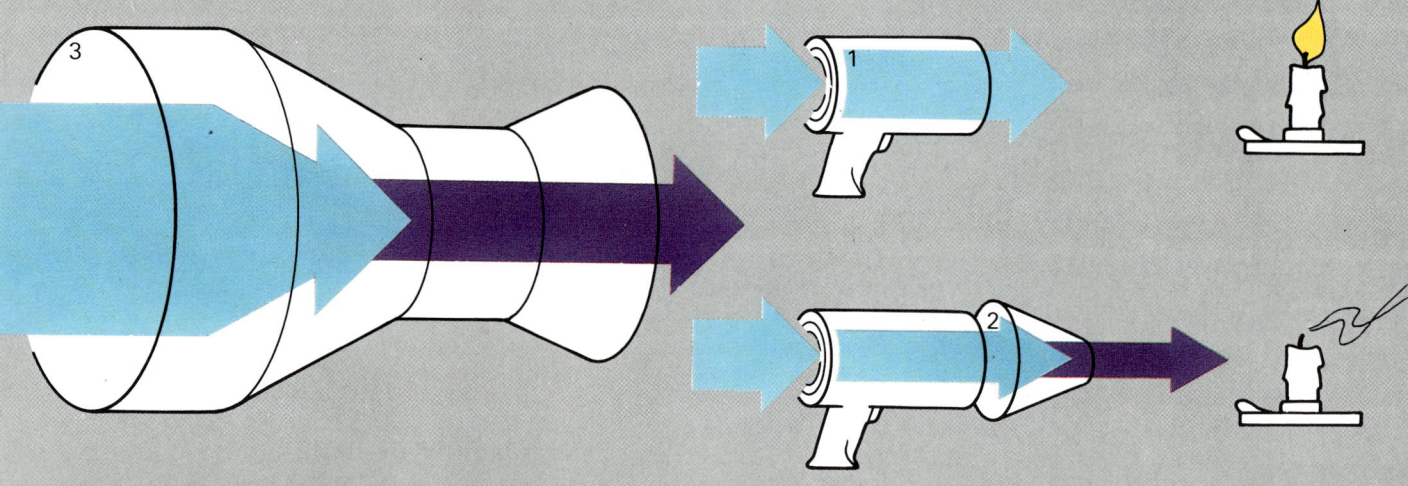

Strengthening a sheet
A sheet of thin card (1) has little strength in itself. Roll it into a tube around two jar lids (2) and it is easily bent (3). But glue strip-shaped ribs of thick cardboard to it (4) and it gains strength in one direction. Roll it round rings of thick cardboard (5) for strength in the other direction. It is now very difficult to bend or crush (6), like an airliner's fuselage (page 12).

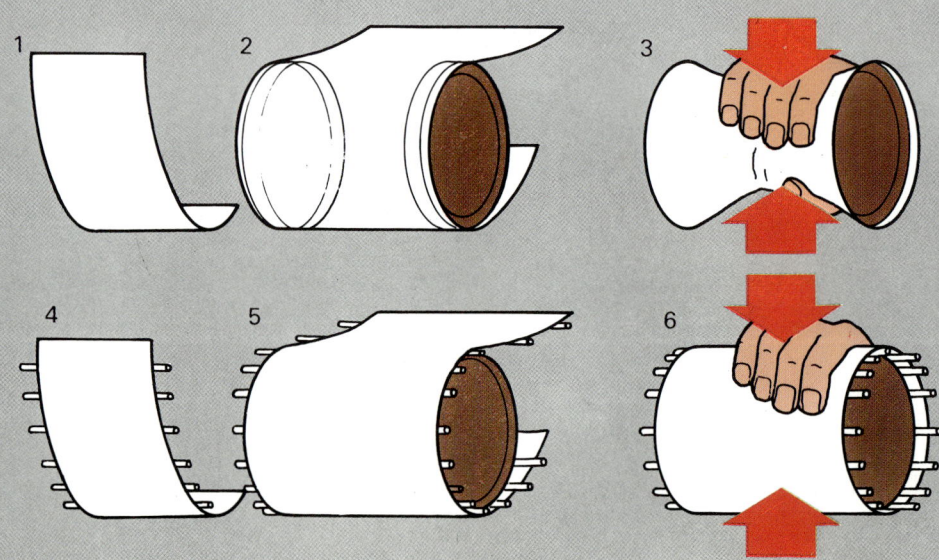

WATFORD GRAMMAR SCHOOL
FULLER MEMORIAL.
LIBRARY

Lifting wings

An aerofoil is the shape of the wing when seen from the side: the front (leading edge) is rounded, the upper surface (1) is more curved than the lower surface (2), and the rear (trailing edge) is tapered. As the wing moves forwards, air passes over the upper and lower surfaces. Because of the greater curve of the upper surface, it moves faster here (3). Faster-moving air creates a lower pressure above the wing compared to below it. The result is a force that "sucks" the wing upwards (4), so lifting the plane.

At low speeds, flaps are extended (5) to increase the lift and the drag. This means the airliner can fly at lower speeds without stalling.

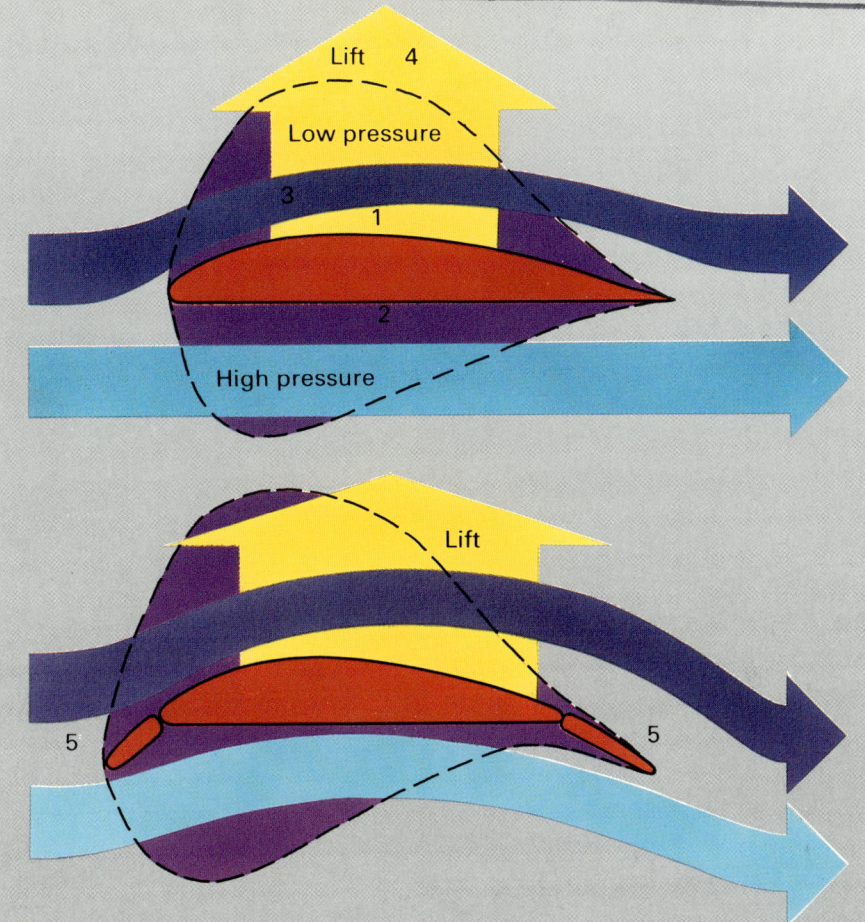

Control surfaces

A plane's control surfaces on its wings, tailplane and tailfins make it go in the direction which the pilot chooses. You can show the principles behind the banking manoeuvre, which turns a plane to the left or right, using a piece of paper. Make a small cut near one corner (1) and fold this down at an angle of about 45 degrees. Then blow gently along the paper (2). The resistance of the folded part against the airstream should push that side of the paper upwards (3). A plane's ailerons, near the tips of its wings, work in the same way. They cause the wings to tilt, so sending the plane into a banked turn to right or left (pages 5 and 14).

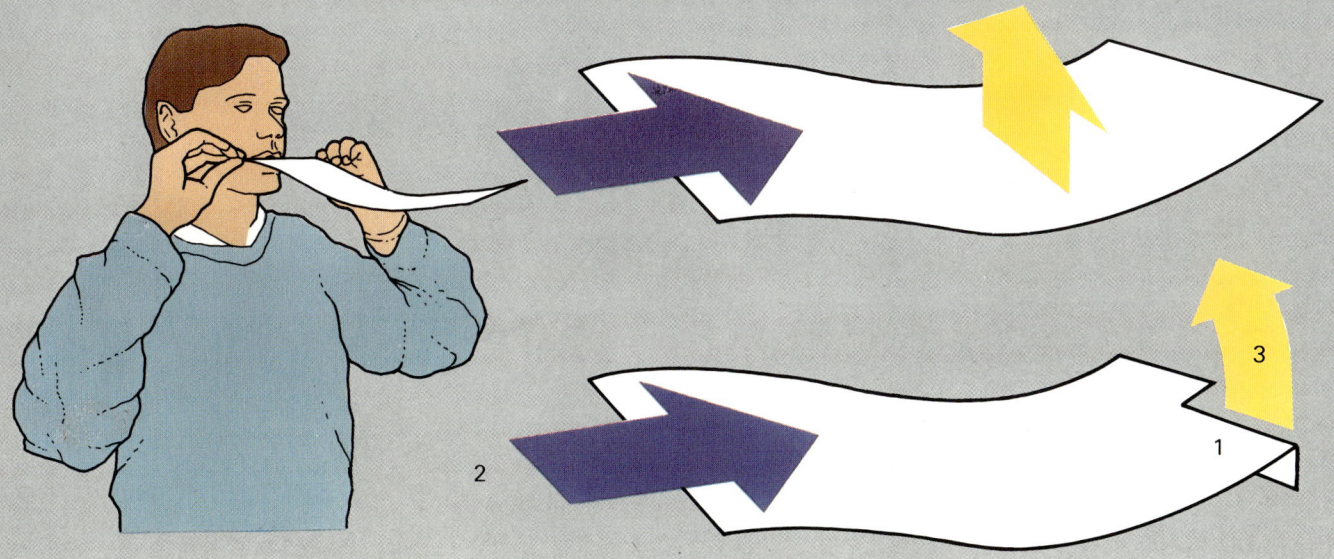

AROUND THE WORLD

Airliners come and go, but the demands on the engineer stay the same: greater safety, better economy, increased reliability, less noise and pollution, better passenger comfort, more navigational aids, less room for pilot error . . . Not only this, but all these requirements must be met while at the same time making sure the manufacturer makes a profit. For the airline business cannot run on "fresh air". The customers pay, and if they are not satisfied, the next time they may choose another airliner. Shown here are some of the biggest-selling airliners of today, in the colours of the world's major airlines. Who knows what tomorrow will bring? The engineers!

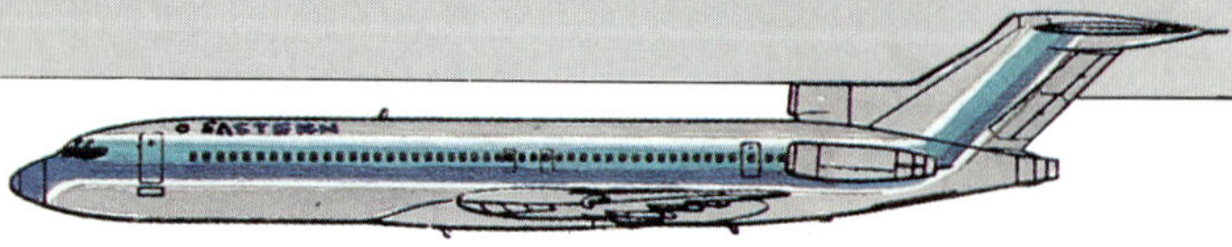

Aeroflot

This Soviet airline is the world's largest in terms of passengers carried and kilometres covered. The communist system means that each major industry, including airplanes, is run by the state.

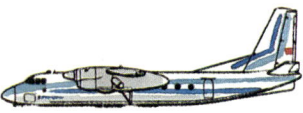

Antonov AN-24B

Boeing 727
Eastern Air Lines (USA)

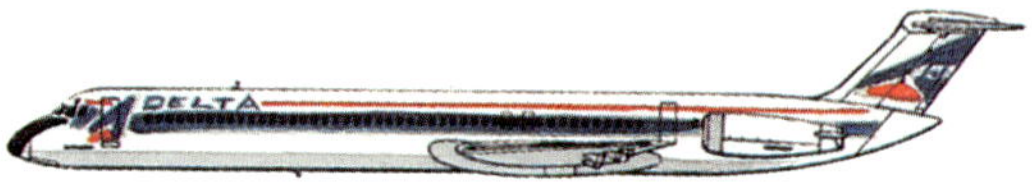

McDonnell-Douglas DC9
Delta Air Lines (USA)

Boeing 737
All-Nippon Airways (Japan)

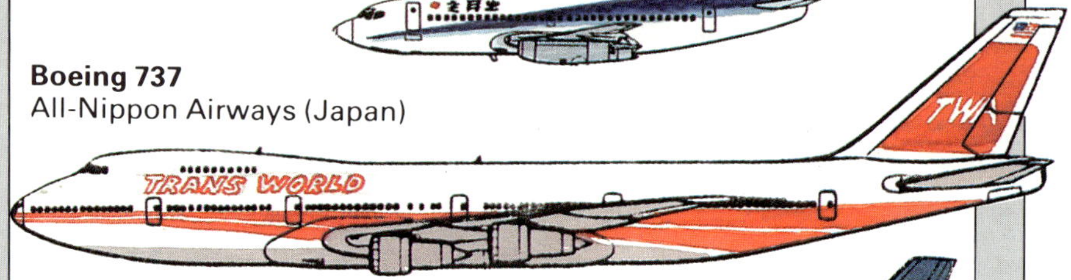

Boeing 747
Trans World Airlines (USA)

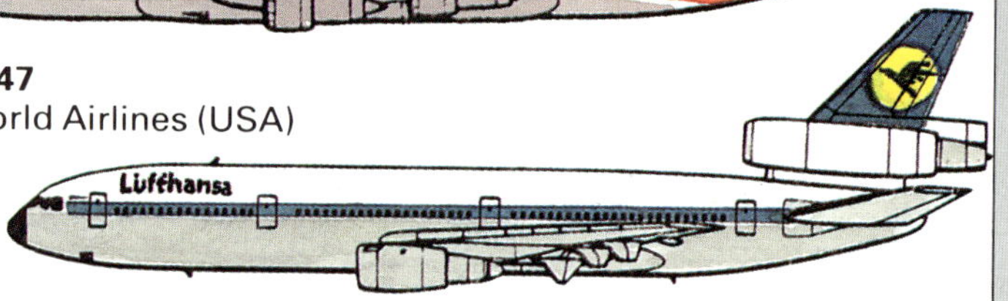

McDonnell-Douglas DC10
Lufthansa German Airlines (West Germany)

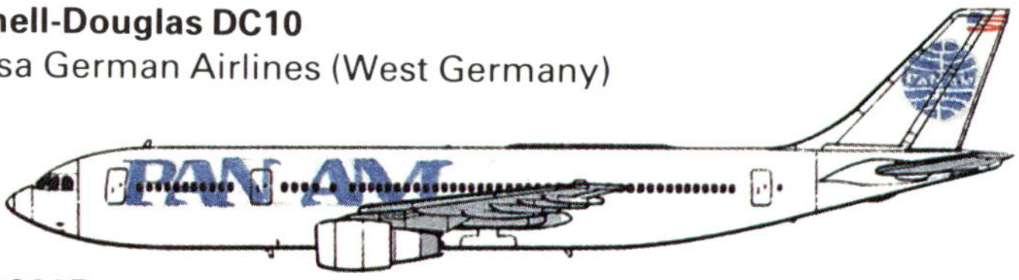

Airbus A300B
Pan American World Airways (USA)

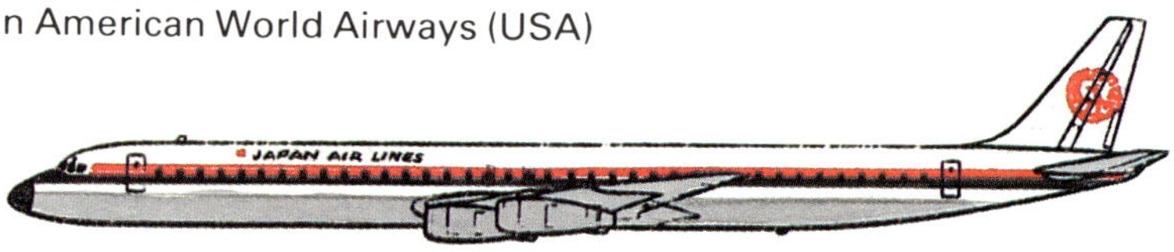

McDonnell-Douglas DC8
Japan Air Lines (Japan)

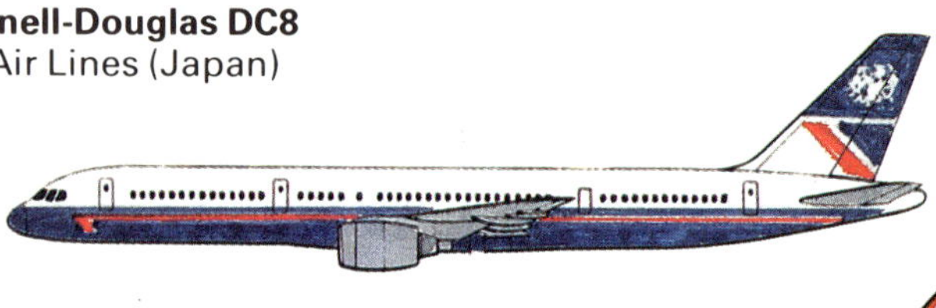

Boeing 757
British Airways (UK)

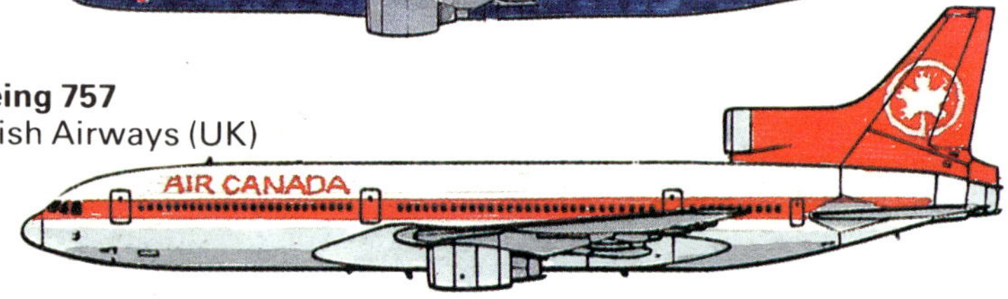

Lockheed Tristar
Air Canada (Canada)

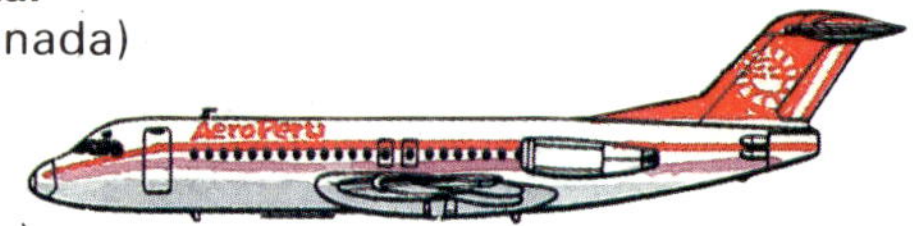

Fokker F28
Aero Peru (Peru)

GLOSSARY

Aileron Hinged control surface on the rear edge of the wing, used to roll the plane or hold the wings level.

Airliner A medium to large plane that carries mainly people.

Autopilot Computer system that can fly the plane without the intervention of the pilot.

Control surface A moveable part of the wing, tailplane or tailfin that alters the airflow past the plane and changes its direction of movement.

Drag The slowing effect on a plane made by the air in front of it being pushed aside.

Elevator The control surface on the tailplane which helps make the plane climb or descend.

Flap A movable part on the wing surface which, when extended on take-off or landing, increases the lift and drag.

Fuselage The main body of a plane; the passenger cabin of a airliner.

Landing gear The wheels and their retractable legs (the "undercarriage").

Pitch The up and down movement of a plane which can be controlled by the elevators on the tailplane.

Propfan A multi-bladed propeller with curved blades which gives the economy of a propeller with the speed of a jet.

Prototype One of the first of a new design of airliner to be built, used as a "guinea pig" for testing and checking before the full production line is set up.

Roll The tilting of a plane from side to side which can be controlled by the ailerons.

Slats Control surfaces at the leading edge of the wing which help increase lift on take-off.

Spoiler The control surface on a plane's wing that destroys lift by disturbing air flow over the wing. It is used to increase drag and so slow the plane.

STOL Short Take-Off and Landing, a plane that can get airborne and land on short runways as found in mountain areas or city centres.

Tailfin The vertical fin on rear end of a plane.

Tailplane The horizontal wing surfaces on the rear end of a plane.

Turbo An engine that uses one or more specially designed, many-bladed fans, called turbines, in its operation.

Turbofan A jet engine which derives extra thrust from a fan which forces large quantities of air past the main engine.

Turbojet A simple jet engine that derives its thrust from expanding exhaust gas.

Turboprop A jet engine with a propeller mounted on the front.

Wingspan The distance from wingtip to wingtip.

Yaw The swivelling movement of a plane to the right or left which can be controlled by the rudder on the tailfin.

WATFORD GRAMMAR SCHOOL
FULLER MEMORIAL
LIBRARY

INDEX

Photographic Credits:
Cover: Austin J. Brown; page 6: Brasilia
Airlines; page 6 (inset) and 10: British
Aerospace; pages 13, 16, 19 (top) and 24:
Airbus Industrie; pages 19 (left and right)
and 20 (all): Boeing; page 23: ICI; page 25:
Lufthansa.

PRINTED IN BELGIUM BY

proost

INTERNATIONAL BOOK PRODUCTION